COLORS OF
Italy

AA Publishing

Author: Nicola Lancaster

Produced by AA Publishing

Published by AA Publishing (a trading name of Automobile Association Developments Limited, whose registered office is Fanum House, Basing View, Basingstoke, Hampshire RG21 4EA; registered number 1878835)

ISBN-10: 0-7495-4238-1
ISBN-13: 978-0-7495-4238-2

A02918

A CIP catalogue record for this book is available from the British Library.

Printed and bound by Leo Paper Group, in China

COLORS OF

Italy

CONT

ENTS

COLORS OF **ITALY**

M y introduction to Italy's mercurial personality came at aged just seven. An idyllic family holiday on the shores of Lake Maggiore was cut short when a terrific storm flooded the campsite and forced us to retreat across the border into Switzerland. That small taste of danger and excitement was enough to ignite my love affair with this varied, unpredictable, and at times frustrating country. But that is Italy for you—a country rich in history, culture, and tradition with a passionate, vivacious, and unpredictable heart.

The boot shape of Italy is instantly recognizable, with the island of Sicily balanced like a football on its toe. The island of Sardinia, in the middle of the Tyrrhenian Sea, lies to the west of the mainland, while several groups of smaller offshore islands line the extensive coastline. The country extends south from the Alps, covering an area of 294,020sq km (113,530sq miles) and has a coastline of 7,600km (4,723 miles). Italy is a long country, covering over 1,500km (930 miles), a contrast to its width, which can be crossed in around 3–4 hours in a car. Every one of its 20 regions has its own special character, landscape, and traditions. Contrary to the picture-postcard image of perpetual sunshine and blue skies, Italy's weather, like its landscape, is variable.

As you travel north to south the scenery gradually shifts from the flat marshy plains of the Veneto and lakes of Lombardy to the gentle, lush green hills and burned red and brown clay soil of Tuscany and Umbria. The greenery soon gives way to the rocky peninsulas of Puglia and Campania and finally fades out to the dry and jagged cliff tops and white, sun-bleached buildings of Calabria, Sicily, and Sardinia. The climate here is dryer and harsher than the well-irrigated north and the soil is generally poorer, making agricultural production difficult.

There is a deep-rooted north–south divide in Italy that dates back to the fall of the Roman Empire. At this time the invasion of the Langobards divided the country into two sections: one "barbarian" and one Byzantine. The north developed into a society open to modernization and innovation, while the history of the south was characterized by exploitation and feudalism. The division was never overcome and is not only visible today in economic and demographic statistics, but also in the relationship between northern and southern Italians. Business and commerce revolve around Milan in the north; while the far south of the country remains one of Europe's most economically depressed areas and northern Italians generally feel that they subsidize the poorer south. The emergence and the success of the Lega Lombarda, a political party campaigning to divide Italy into three federal states, the North, Central, and South, with the North leading the way, is a reflection of the depth of feeling in certain areas. On the positive side, southern Italians work fewer hours and enjoy a lower cost of living than their more frenetic northern counterparts.

The modern republic of Italy was created in 1948 but political life has been both interesting and complicated since, with well over 50 governments being elected to power since World War II. An electoral college drawn from the houses of parliament and regional representatives chooses the President, the head of state. Decision-making lies with the lower house, the Chamber of Deputies, directly elected by universal suffrage. The upper house, the Senate, is made up of six representatives from each region, plus a number of senators-for-life. The seat of national government is in Rome, with the president residing in the Palazzo del Quirinale, the Chamber of Deputies in Palazzo Montecitorio, and the Senate in Palazza Madama, near Piazza Navona. The complicated electoral system, based on proportional representation, has been responsible for a series of coalition governments, which in the past have suffered from corruption at the highest levels. The Mani Pulite (Clean Hands) investigations in the 1990s aimed to bring an end to the culture of bribery and corruption, leading to the downfall of some of the older parties. Scandals continue to be exposed in the press, but in general there is a feeling that Italy is moving forward toward more stable times.

When in Rome...

Architecturally, Italy is a showcase for the building styles of different ages, and nowhere is the range and concentration of styles more evident than in Italy's capital, Rome. Faced for the first time with a view which takes in more than 3,000 years of history it is impossible not to be hopelessly awestruck. Visitors are easily distinguished from the Romans, as they are the ones on the bus whose heads turn to look at the Colosseum as they pass by on the route to the heart of the city.

The best thing to do is surrender and be a tourist for a while—visit the Colosseum, the Vatican Museums, the Galleria Borghese, the Forum, the Spanish Steps, get your photo taken with a gladiator, and join the throng at the Trevi Fountain, throwing two coins over your shoulder into the water; one to ensure that a wish comes true and another to ensure your return to the Eternal City. You won't be doing it alone, but that simply adds to the romance of the experience.

After a while, the novelty of crumbling ruins can wear off but there is so much more to see in Rome beside ancient sites and art galleries. The best way to find the essence of a place is to get lost in it, and Rome is no exception. Some of the most enchanting treasures are found down the

The forum started out as a market and gradually evolved into the political, economic and religious focus of ancient Rome. It is now one of the city's most important archaeological sites, with monuments spanning 2,000 years of history.

wonderfully shabby side streets, such as the green-shuttered buildings painted in peeling and faded shades of terracotta, pink, and yellow, an artist's dream. It is difficult to get bored with so much living street theater at every turn. Marvel as you watch mopeds wobble and weave though stalls piled high with fruit and vegetables in Piazza Campo dei Fiori, handlebars laden with shopping bags spilling over with purchases. With a simple breakfast of fruit collected from the market, retire to a suitable vantage point overlooking a square, and wait for the show to begin, drinking in the smell of morning coffee wafting from the awakening cafés and basking in the morning sun as it begins to peep over the birch trees lining the streets.

Off the Beaten Track

With so many famous artistic and historic cities to explore it is easy to understand why some people overlook the opportunity to venture off the beaten track, but Italy has some of the best wilderness areas in Europe and the rewards for seeking them out are high. Italy now has 20 national parks, with more being established all the time, and well over 400 smaller nature reserves, natural parks, and wetland areas. National parks cover just over 1.5 million ha and make up five percent of the country, with the aim of reaching 10 percent in the future. The Gran Paradiso is Italy's oldest national park, covering three valleys; Cogne, Valsavarenche, and Val de Rhêmes around the Gran Paradiso mountain range, famous for its chamois, ibex, and mountain flowers. The Parco Nazionale d'Abruzzo is the third-largest national park in Italy and straddles three regions, Abruzzo, Lazio, and

Markets are the first port of call for fresh produce. Most of the larger towns have a daily market where people can catch up on the local gossip, while supporting local producers.

Molise. It is also home to rare species, and the wild Apennine landscape and mountains provide the ideal habitat for Marsicano brown bears, golden eagles, Apennine wolves, and chamois deer.

Natural Resources

Italy has very few natural resources apart from natural gas, and no substantial deposits of oil, iron, or coal. With the exception of a few fertile areas, much of the land is unsuited to agriculture and so Italy imports much of its food. Although 1.4 million people are employed in farming, only 28 percent of Italy is arable and most farms are small, with the average being only 7ha (17 acres). The country's economic strengths lie in the processing and manufacturing of goods, primarily in small or medium-sized family-owned firms. The major industries are car and precision machinery manufacture, textiles, clothing and footwear, ceramic and chemical production, and food processing. Tourism continues to prosper, bringing in around 13 percent of the national income, and 62 percent of the population is employed in the travel and service industries. Italy's famous landmarks are now iconic

Top left: Michaelangelo carved his 13-foot high statue of David from a single piece of marble quarried from the mountains of Carrara in Tuscany.
Top right: The town of Pariana in the foothills of the Alpi Apuane mountain range.
Next page: The town of Ravello in Campania.

marketing tools—St Peter's Basilica in Rome, the Leaning Tower of Pisa, the Duomo in Florence, all repeatedly reproduced on postcards and merchandise, are a valuable national commodity.

It is olive oil, however, that is now Italy's most valuable export. The ancient olive trees that produce the oil are now so desirable as decoration for gardens abroad and in the north of the country, that legislation has been introduced to prevent them from being stolen by unscrupulous dealers and sold to private 'collectors'.

With a possible lifespan of up to 2,000 years, the hardy evergreen olive trees can withstand the battering of storms, salt water, extremes of temperature, and extended periods of drought. Where many other trees have died, the olive has always survived. These trees can be neglected for years and then brought back into production, yielding fruit in even the harshest conditions, outliving humans, and generating income for future generations. These characteristics have made them an attractive investment for centuries and planting an olive grove in a garden in Italy can still add significant financial value to a property.

Olive-leaf extract has anti-bacterial, anti-viral, and anti-fungal properties and recent studies have shown that eating olive oil can help to lower cholesterol and reduce the risk of heart attacks and certain cancers. This hardy tree, which embodies the spirit of Italy, not only looks good, it also lasts for centuries and bears delicious, life-enhancing fruit.

Grand Passions

Apart from architecture and food, opera is another great draw for visitors to Italy. The season runs from November to May and if you are lucky you may stumble across a festival or a live performance in a piazza—the perfect opportunity to hear Italian opera as it should be sung, on home ground to an enthusiastic crowd. Sleepy squares are transformed into open-air theaters, filled with rows of regimental chairs facing a stage often backed by a *duomo*—the perfect backdrop, beautifully lit with soft-colored lights and with classical images projected on to its facade.

Italy has contributed much to Western music over the centuries. It was an Italian monk, Guido d'Arezzo, who devised the musical scale and a Venetian printer, Ottavino Petrucci, who invented a method of printing music in 1501, an industry that Italy dominated for years. This explains why musicians still play *allegro* and *forte* today. The piano is originally from Italy, the accordion was invented in the Marches, and the beautiful violins of the Guarneri and Stradivarius of Cremona have set a standard in instrument-making that has never been beaten. Venice gave birth to talents such as Antonio Vivaldi (1678–1741), a composer passed over in his own day, but now celebrated for his major work the *Four Seasons*.

In musical terms, though, Italy is most famous for being the birthplace of opera. Its roots date back to the 16th century and the Florentine academy known as the Camerata. Mozart, although not

Carnevale is traditionally the time when Venetians let their hair down before giving up pleasures for Lent. The party lasts for ten days and the entire city is taken over by masked Venetians attending balls and parading through the streets.

Italian, wrote three Italian operas, *Don Giovanni, Così fan tutte*, and *Le Nozze di Figaro*. The golden age of Italian opera came at the end of the 19th century with Giuseppe Verdi's (1813–1901) romantic works such as *Aida, Rigoletto, Nabucco*, and *La Traviata* form the bedrock of the operatic canon, while Giacomo Puccini (1858–1924) brought the medium up to date by adding a touch of realism to operas such as *Tosca* and *Madame Butterfly*.

The most prestigious opera house is La Scala in Milan, but Milan's operatic tradition is in its infancy when compared with that of Naples and Venice. There are plenty of elaborate opera houses in Rome, but some of the best and most romantic venues are out in the open air, in piazzas, ancient amphitheaters, and arenas. However, nothing can beat opera performed in an ancient Roman site, such as the summer festival in the baths of Caracalla. This is opera on a grand scale with horses and elephants often appearing in performances. You need to book well in advance—and take a cushion.

Italian Character

It is almost a given that every town will have a smoky bar or café reserved for the male population, the seating plan impenetrable to visitors and governed by a hidden hierarchy based on respect and trust earned over a long period of time. You won't have to go far to find a square where you can sit and observe from a distance groups of men banging their fists on the table tops, passionately involved in a debate.

For Italians communication is paramount and it takes more than a language barrier to prevent the message from getting across. This openness and need to express opinions extends to visitors and as a result, if you are prepared to make an effort, there are very few situations where you will be unable to make yourself understood. Of course some embarrassing misunderstandings arise—order *una pasta* (a cake) instead of *la pasta* (pasta) in a café for example and you will end up getting something slightly sweeter than you had bargained for—but it is amazing how much you can convey with a few basic Italian phrases and the use of body language.

Italians are eager to entertain and their social embrace is wide reaching. One thing you will find in abundance is an unending supply of hospitality, generosity, and good will. Visitors to Italy quickly find that there is far more to Italian food than pasta and pizza. Meal times are as much about socializing as eating. The interior of the local *trattoria* is like a family dining room with an atmosphere to match. Plate after plate of delicious homemade antipasti, pasta, and fish dishes are served up, the wineglasses seem bottomless and just when you think you couldn't possibly eat another thing, the restaurateur's wife comes out with a huge dish filled with layered tiramisu and the party continues into the early hours of the morning. This talent for extending warm welcomes makes visitors feel immediately at home and encourages them to return time and time again.

The term *al fresco* literally means 'in the open air' and refers to theatre as well as dining. These diners (right) in Florence have a view of the River Arno and the *duomo*.

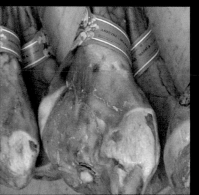

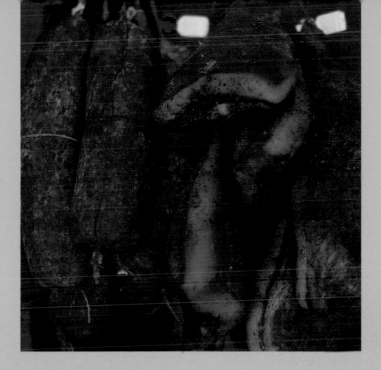

THE ITALIAN DELI

Eating is one of the biggest pleasures in Italy. The diversity of the country is as apparent in its food as it is in its cities, culture, and landscape. The arrival of the year's 'first' is eagerly awaited and welcomed in the restaurants, food stores, and markets and is celebrated with festivals.

There is no such thing as Italian cooking; rather, there is Tuscan, Roman, Bolognese, Milanese, Neapolitan...and so on. Fresh ingredients are the key and each region's cooking is dictated by the local produce available in the area—rice in the regions near the River Po, truffles in Piedmont and Umbria, beans and pulses in Tuscany, and a vast array of fish and seafood in the coastal areas.

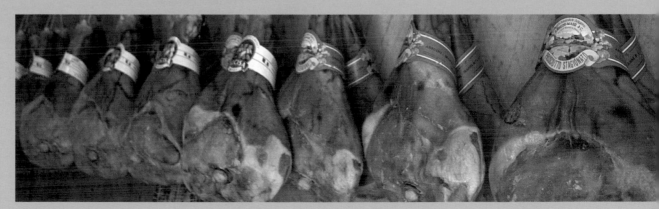

Lard was once a poor man's food, referred to as 'anarchist chow' after the partisans of Colonnata who survived solely on a diet of pork fat preserved in salt when they fled with their pigs into the Apuane Alps following the 1859 uprising against the invading Austrians. Today the region's lard,

Lardo di Colonnata, is a delicacy and its production has been refined and perfected. It is made with fat from the back of the pig and is prepared by cutting off and treating individual slabs with salt and cinnamon. The slabs are then immersed in brine and placed inside vessels made from locally

quarried marble, then slowly seasoned with herbs and spices and left for six months to mature in a controlled climate. When it is ready, the white or slightly pink *lardo* is cut into slices and served on hot toast or used to add intense, smoky overtones to sauces.

POMODORI &
PINENUTS

Italian cooking is straightforward, its quality dictated by the superlative standard of fresh ingredients available. Food shopping is a daily social event and most provincial and regional capitals have daily food markets selling meat, fish, dairy produce, fruit, and vegetables.

There are many varieties of pomodori (tomatoes), each with its own distinct taste and character. The tangy Roman variety, locally known as casalini, is deeply wrinkled and small. Campania's variety are smaller still, only slightly bigger than cherry tomatoes, and known as pomodori dasperferani

while the tomatoes in Sicily are large, perfectly round, and sweet. At the end of the season in the south, the last of the tomatoes on the vine are cut down and hung in a cool part of the house to ensure there is a constant source of the ripe red fruit available throughout the winter.

Basil is the herb of choice in Italy, a perfect partner to the tomato. Its aromatic leaves, combined with a touch of garlic, can lift a simple sauce and transform a basic dish into something special.

Pinenuts, tiny cream pine kernels, are traditionally crushed by hand with a pestle and mortar and combined with garlic, basil, olive oil, and a hard white cheese such as *parmigiano reggiano*, to create the deep green pesto sauce native to Liguria, and now popular worldwide.

As well as nuts, many types of beans are combined with pasta, especially in soups. Chickpeas and berlotti beans are the most popular choice. Berlotti beans are plump and their pale pinkish-brown skin is flecked with burgundy, but black-eyed beans, white with a black blotch, have a more distinctive taste.

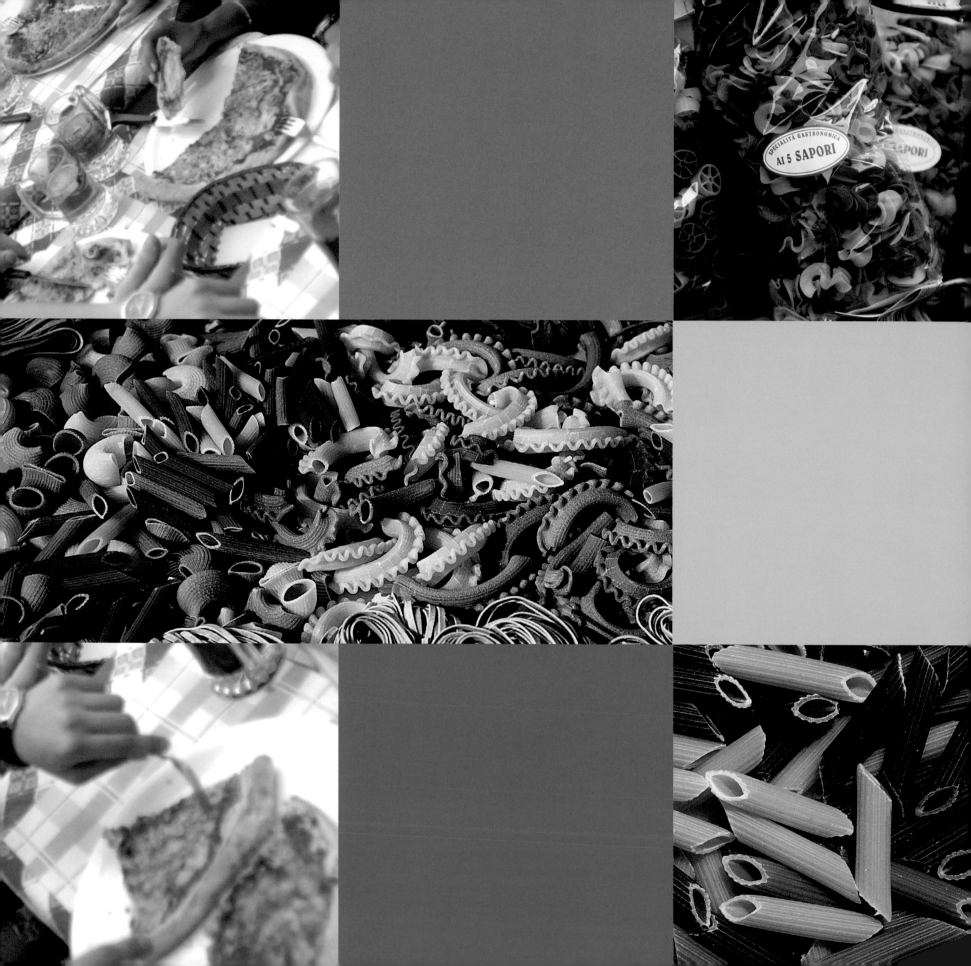

The unique textures and tastes of Italian cheeses have been refined over centuries. There is a huge number of varieties, their characters influenced by factors such as the quality of the soil, the climate, humidity, and the forage available to the indigenous breeds of cows, goats, and sheep.

FORMAGGIO

Cheeses produced using similar methods can differ in taste immensely from region to region, reflecting the unique character of each area. Their intense, often sweet aromas are guaranteed to attract you into delicatessens and local shops throughout the country. The golden and white *parmigiano reggiano* (Parmesan), a hard, cows'-milk cheese primarily used for grating, is a vital ingredient in many Italian dishes. Its origins can be traced back seven centuries to the provinces of Parma, Reggio Emilia, Modena, parts of Bologna, and Matova (Mantua).

OLIVES
& GRAPES

The evergreen olive tree lives for an average of 300 to 600 years in southern Italy and can live as long as 2,000 years. The load-bearing branches spread out over time and contort into a variety of gnarled and twisted shapes. Owning an ancient olive tree has become something of a status symbol in the fashion-conscious north. So sought-after are these trees that some specimens are fetching up to €5,000 at top designer garden outlets. Sadly, many of the uprooted and relocated trees fail to survive their first winter. The inflated prices have not gone unnoticed by those in the criminal fraternity, sparking a wave of dawn raids on olive groves in the south. Farmers have to seek permission from the government before uprooting their oldest trees, but that hasn't stopped many producers of poor-quality olive oil from cashing in on the latest trend.

SEAFOOD

The Rialto market near the Ponte di Rialto in Venice is one of the most famous fish markets in Italy and the waters of the lagoon and the Adriatic Sea yield a diverse catch.
Piles of coral-pink prawns, mounds of whitebait and blue-grey mussels, and row upon row of seabream, seabass, and sardines are laid out for the locals to choose from six days a week, their shiny silver-blue scales glistening in the early morning light. Venetians arrive early to choose the best specimens particularly the more unusual species found in the local waters—local specialties include *granceole* (spider crab) drizzled with oil and lemon, *spaghetti al vongole* (spaghetti with clams) and *sepie* (cuttlefish), used, along with its ink, in risotto. Risotto with squid ink is a dish particularly favored by the Milanese.
In addition to the sea, Italy also has many lakes,

filled with freshwater fish. Stuffed tench served with polenta is the main dish available in the restaurants along the shores of Lago d'Iseo, while trout and eel are served with plenty of olive oil and aromatic herbs around Lago di Garda. Fish has been preserved here for centuries and

there are many different methods. Dried bleak is salted in the open air and then packed into glass jars filled with brine between June and July on the western coast of Lago di Garda. Whole twaite shad, are caught in May in the lakes, cleaned, threaded on to string and then dried in the sun before being

pressed into layers, covered in olive oil and then later eaten with a dash of vinegar. The area around Brescia, a town in the north of Italy, is known for the eggs of white sturgeon, a fish which has been farmed here since Roman times.

FUNGHI

Porcini mushrooms, the wild ceps or boletus mushrooms commonly used in Italian cooking, are large with a shiny brown top, honeycombed underside and a rich, meaty taste.
The most sought-after *funghi* though are white truffles. Known as 'fruit of the woods' these *funghi* grow underground around the roots of oaks, poplars, hazelnut trees, and certain pines in Piedmont, Romagna, the Marches, and Tuscany. Difficult to find and extremely expensive as a result, they retail at around €700–€1,000 per kilo. Their value means that there are laws governing collection and collectors must be licensed and part of a co-operative to hunt out the prized delicacies. Pigs and dogs are used to sniff them out, but dogs are preferred to pigs, who have a tendency to eat the truffles. For the taste without the expense, try truffle oil, olive oil infused with truffle.

LIFE & PEOPLE

COLORS OF ITALY: **LIFE & PEOPLE**

The population of Italy is around 57.8 million and the country has some of the most densely populated areas in Europe. As well as having a strong sense of national pride, Italians also remain loyal to their regional roots and identify firstly with their region, Tuscany or Umbria for example, a feeling that dates back to a time when Italy was a number of individual countries.

Unified today, Italy is still divided into 20 regions, each its own characteristics, reflecting the diversity of the country, both in its landscape and culture. Such variety makes Italy a great place for people-watching and it is fascinating to sit back and while away a few hours observing daily life unfold before your eyes. Italians love to play to an audience and often move in crowds—the city streets are the stage, the piazzas the perfect place for showing off.

In Italy's past, the families of the bride and groom often arranged marriages. Things are far more relaxed these days, but marriage is still a family affair and there are many customs and traditions that help to make the wedding day a success. On the day of the wedding, it is bad luck for the bride

LATIN LOVERS

to wear any gold until the wedding ring has been slipped onto her finger—gold engagement rings are removed well before the service. It is also unlucky to marry during Lent and Advent and the months of May and August are best avoided—May is a month reserved for the Virgin Mary, and

August is thought to invite bad luck. Sunday, though, is considered the luckiest day to get married. It may not be ideal for the wedding photos, but families often pray for rain on the wedding day as it is believed that a wet bride is a lucky bride—'*Sposa bagnata, sposa fortunata.*'

RELIGIOUS ROBES

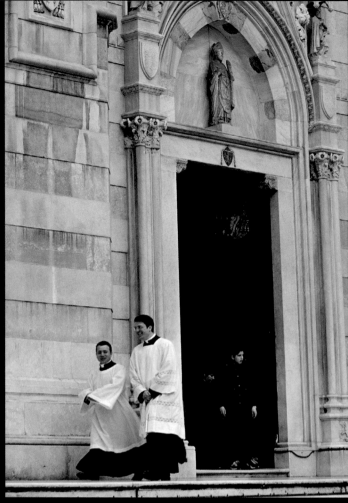

Around 85 percent of native-born Italians are
nominally Catholic, and celebrations such as First
Communion remain a major event. Still important,
too, is the tradition of *onomastico*, celebrating
your saint's day (the saint who shares your first
name) as you would your own birthday.

Catholic priests, nuns, and pilgrims from all over the world travel to the Vatican for the opportunity to celebrate Mass in the Basilica di San Pietro, often a lifetime's dream. Every morning, priests of every nationality occupy the altars of the chapels within the basilica, saying Mass in dozens of languages to accommodate the many nationalities of the worshippers. Confessions are heard in different languages too. A red light over a confessional indicates that it is 'open for business', and a sign informs the penitents which languages the priest speaks.

The Catholic Church is making an effort to move with the times. The Pope introduced a 'thought for the day' SMS text-messaging service, and a Trieste priest decided to open his church on Saturday nights until 2am to attract weary clubbers.

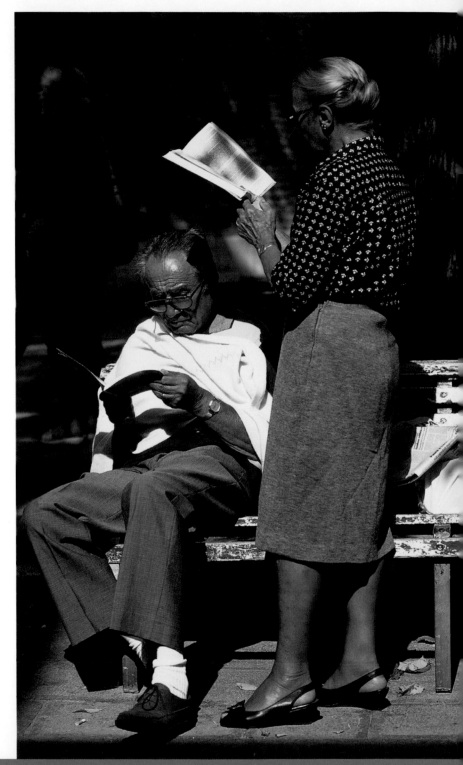

Previous page: The Vatican is still a popular place for pilgrimage and the Pope continues to give weekly public Masses, which draw huge crowds to Piazza San Pietro.

The stereotypical image of the pasta-serving Italian Mamma surrounded by a houseful of kids is way off the mark today. Women's roles are evolving, particularly in the north, with many women now continuing their careers after marriage. Over the last 20 years the birthrate has fallen alarmingly, while the divorce rate has rocketed, affecting traditional family roles and social patterns. Worryingly, Italy has one of the lowest birthrates in the world, at 9.1 per 1,000 inhabitants, and one of the lowest fertility rates with 1.2 children born per adult woman, compared with 2.0 in the USA.

YOUNG & OLD

Despite the pressures of the modern world, family and community ties remain strong. It is estimated that 56 percent of people aged between 25 and 29 still live at home and the number is increasing.

The impression of the family gathering together regularly is still a very real one—51 percent of Italians live within 15 minutes of their mother's home—and the concept of loyalty continues to underpin all Italian relationships, whether it is between blood relations or friends.

Caffè del Greco

Italy's piazzas and wide streets are perfectly suited to alfresco dining, and as soon as the weather allows, the diners and the tables and chairs move outside—what better way to enjoy a meal or a coffee on a balmy evening than while watching the world go by?

Italian coffee is made using the espresso method. In bars, freshly ground coffee beans are put into a filter compressed, and attached to the machine. Hot, not boiling, water is forced through the freshly ground coffee, producing an intense, aromatic brew with a distinctive *crema* (cream)

on top. Milk is frothed with steam and added to a shot of espresso for the perfect cappuccino. The original Italian cappuccino is served lukewarm in a small cup, unlike the hot, frothy varieties served in styrofoam cups in coffee shops elsewhere.

The roast of the beans varies from region to region, becoming increasingly potent the further south you go. Italians will tell you that the best place to have coffee is Rome, because of the superior quality of the water.

As Italians gravitate toward the cities, reluctantly leaving their native regions behind for economic reasons, it is becoming harder to maintain the traditional rural way of life. The *agriturismo* scheme, particularly popular in Tuscany and Umbria, provides money for farmers and landowners to maintain redundant farm buildings by converting them into holiday accommodation. This can take the form of a small luxurious hotel, an apartment with kitchen, or simply a handful of rooms in a converted barn. They are often in beautiful, unspoiled surroundings and frequently provide activities such as horse back riding, fishing, escorted walking, and mountain bike tours. The aim is to bring money to the community at the same time as giving visitors the chance to relax in beautiful countryside and catch a glimpse of rural Italian life.

Next page: At the Murano glass factory the centuries-old tradition of glass-making is as strong as ever, with glass of every size, shape, and color available.

STREETLIFE

In the evening across the country, Italians take to the streets for a stroll. The *passeggiata* (as it is known) is a national ritual, a chance to get out and mingle, debate local current affairs, and exchange the day's stories and gossip.

Although it is a relaxed affair, plenty of posing goes on, prompted by a desire to see and be seen. Well-groomed and impeccably dressed with not a hair out of place, couples put on their sunglasses and step outside for a chance to show off their style and check out the competition.

Families parade their children and newborn babies with pride, while young men and women shine their shoes, fix their hair and put on their best, head-turning outfits, reveling in the attention.

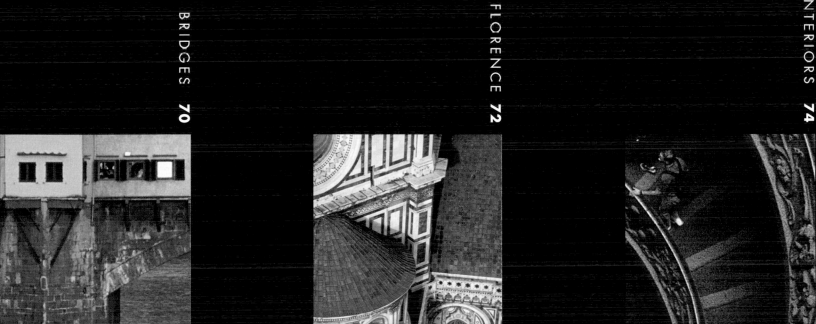

ROME

It is not always easy living with history. Monuments can get in the way of modern life, as with the Forum in Rome, which occupies a prime piece of *centro storico* (historic center) real estate. Romans are so used to living among ancient sites that they no longer give the Colosseum a second look and kids grow up playing football around the ruins, using tumbledown columns for goal posts. The city's inadequate two-line subway system cannot be extended because digging under the streets of Rome invariably leads to the discovery of yet more ruins.

Italy's artistic and architectural heritage, which spans more than 4,000 years, comprises archaeological sites, monuments, churches, and works of art. In the last 50 years, the country has restored many buildings, preserving important treasures nationwide. The ongoing process of decay and the cost of restoration are daunting and many regions contain abandoned towns or villages, churches that have been looted and stand empty and scaffolding-clad buildings that remain covered for years.

Despite the challenges, Italy has more than 30 Unesco World Heritage Sites and stands at the top of the international list, recognized as the country with the highest number of sites of cultural importance. Visitors can easily come across an archaeological dig or discover a wonderful baroque church in the central piazza of what appears to be a tiny, unassuming village. Wherever you go in the country, it is impossible to ignore the wealth of artistic and architectural treasures, which are evidence of Italy's many previous cultures, ruling families, and lost civilizations.

The writer and historian Georgina Masson summed up how Rome lives with its past when she referred to the city as a sheet of parchment used over and over again, with the new text written over the faded original or squeezed in between the lines. Every city has a past, but Rome has more overwriting than other cities, and far fewer rubbings-out. Nowhere else will you find such a concentration of architectural styles, from the ruins of imperial Rome to the glories of the Vatican, and from the sculptural masterpieces of the baroque to the golden age of the Renaissance.

CHURCHES

The Romans invented the architectural form of the basilica, a great hall where the central, higher space, lit by clerestory windows, was divided from the side aisles by rows of columns. Basilicas were

Previous page: Basilica di San Marco in Venice.

impressive structures with exterior porticoes and colonnades, but they were essentially practical buildings where crowds could gather in comfort. Cool and airy during the stifling summer months, they were principally used as meeting places for business and for judicial proceedings.

RUINS & REMAINS

It is hard not to be awestruck by some of Italy's best-preserved sites, such as Taormina's *Teatro Greco* (Greek Theater) in Sicily, which held up to 5,400 spectators. It has a view of the sea, with snow-capped Mount Etna in the background, and it is easy to imagine a masked performance of a Greek tragedy taking place on the stage below.

TOWERS

Pisa's famous Leaning Tower is the exception rather than the rule and Italy has many impressive examples of perpendicular towers across the country. The *campanile*, or bell tower, is an essential part of even the smallest town, traditionally used to bring a community together or raise the alarm. Belltowers were also important strategic lookout points, a necessity during unstable times when it paid to keep an eye on the neighbors. Visitors to hilltop towns in medieval times were impressed by the architectural detail and size of these towers. By 1150 the Italians were winning the race to pierce the skies, their construction techniques unmatched by any other country in the world and only beaten when the Americans rose to the challenge in the 1900s. San Gimignano in Tuscany (above left) is nicknamed 'Medieval Manhattan' after the towers that pierce

its skyline. The town flourished during the Middle Ages, but its population split into factions, divided over their allegiance to the Pope or the empire. During years of conflict and a frenzy of competitive construction, the town's rival wealthy families built 72 defensive towers as a symbol of their dominance over the other families, 14 of which are still standing today. The tallest, the Torre Grossa, is 54m (175ft) high.

At 99m high (325ft), the redbrick copper-roofed *campanile* in Piazza San Marco in Venice (above) is even bigger. Built in 1514, the bell tower also served as a lighthouse for the lagoon and remained standing until 1902 when it collapsed. No-one was hurt, but the custodian's cat was killed. The tower was painstakingly rebuilt *Com'era, dov'era* (like it was, where it was) and it was reopened in 1912.

PIAZZAS

Piazzas can be found at the heart of almost every town, usually with a central fountain or monument and lined with restaurants and cafés, such as the Campo in Siena (above). They provide a venue for markets and festivities and are popular meeting places and open-air areas in which to relax.

The elongated Piazza Navona in Rome was laid out in the 17th century and follows the shape of Domitian's stadium (AD86), an outdoor venue for games, athletics, festivals, and in the 15th century even jousting. It is now a popular meeting place and is famous for its three fountains and baroque

sculptural masterpieces by Bernini. Compared to the narrow side streets, the sheer scale of Piazza San Marco in Venice (right), is breathtaking. It was described as 'the biggest drawing room in Europe' by Napoleon and is lined on three sides by arcades.

BRIDGES

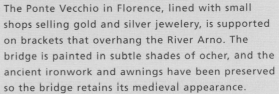

The Ponte Vecchio in Florence, lined with small shops selling gold and silver jewelery, is supported on brackets that overhang the River Arno. The bridge is painted in subtle shades of ocher, and the ancient ironwork and awnings have been preserved so the bridge retains its medieval appearance.

Florence was the birthplace of the Renaissance and
the focus of creative activity for some of the
world's greatest artistic talents. The city's churches
and museums contain familiar masterpieces, while
the narrow streets are lined with splendid palaces
and elegant shops.

FLORENCE

The sublime, if somewhat grimy, Duomo of Santa Maria del Fiore is vast, its green and white marble exterior and terracotta, domed roofs dominating the city skyline. Beside it is the *campanile* (left), covered with bands of green, white, and pink marble and decorated with sculptures and reliefs showing prophets, patriarchs, and scenes from the Old Testament. A climb up 414 steps brings you to the top where there are outstanding 360-degree views of the city and surrounding Tuscan hills.

INTERIORS

The ultimate expression of interior decoration to come out of Italy is the fresco, a method of applying paint to the walls so that the pigment becomes a permanent part of it, resulting in a long-lasting image. The artist first draws the image on paper, then expands the drawing to the desired size to make the work cartoon. The outline of the figures is then pricked out with tiny holes and the cartoon is attached to the wall. Renaissance artists then blew charcoal dust through the holes, leaving the outline of the picture on the wall when the cartoon was removed. Pigments are then applied to wet plaster. As the plaster dries a chemical reaction takes place, leaving a permanent picture. Often the interior of buildings and churches in Italy is just as dramatic as the exterior. This spiral staircase (right) is in the Vatican.

& VIEW

COLORS OF ITALY: **LANDMARKS & VIEWS**

4

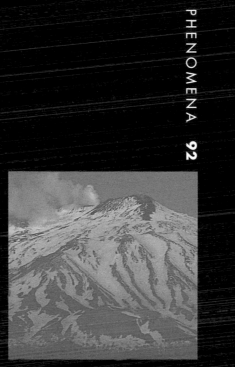

PISA

Travel through Italy and you will quickly become acquainted with a range of contrasting landscapes from dramatic mountain ranges and marshy plains to dense woodlands and plateaux. North of Genoa lie the flat plains of the Po Valley, fertile and intensively farmed. These mist-laden flatlands are backed by the Alps, stretching eastward from the border with France at Ventimiglia through to Slovenia, with the most scenic ranges, the Ortles and Dolomites, in the east.

Geologically different from the rest of the Alps, the Dolomites were once coral reefs, formed beneath the seabed 250 million years ago and uplifted 190 million years later. Wind, ice, and storms shaped the pinky-orange limestone into unique formations of pinnacles and needle-sharp peaks. This is an area of breathtaking natural beauty where turquoise lakes in fertile green valleys reflect the dark fir trees and stark jagged peaks which tower above.

There are man-made wonders too, from ancient monumental buildings to tiny, densely-packed medieval hilltop towns and grand churches, often with high towers from which to take in the surrounding view.

The Torre Pendente (Leaning Tower), a striking cathedral, and Italy's largest baptistery all stand together in the Campo dei Miracoli in Pisa. The foundations of the tower were laid on sandy soil in 1173 and the structure began to lean long before it was finished. By 1284 the tilt was 90cm (35in) from the vertical and by the time the tower was completed in 1350, it had increased to 1.45m (4.75ft). In 1990 a team of engineers attached tons of lead to the north side, fixing them with steel cables. The tower began to settle and within five months it had stabilized.

THE COLOSSEUM

Built nearly 2,000 years ago, the Colosseum in Rome was the largest amphitheater built by the Roman Empire and it is now the largest surviving ancient Roman structure in the world. In places, all four floors are still intact, while the middle is filled with a jumble of ruins, all that's left of the labyrinthine network of passages beneath the gladiatorial arena. The channels were used to hold men and beasts as well as acting as water conduits when the arena was flooded for *naumachia*. Here criminals fought to the death in re-enactments of naval battles on scaled-down galleys.

THE LAKES

The largest of Italy's lakes, Lago di Garda, is 51km (32 miles) long and 17km (11 miles) across at its widest point. It is renowned for its clear waters, warm enough to swim in during the summer months. Mediterranean flora including olive and citrus trees flourishes here in the warm climate, and the lakeside promenades are lined with palm trees and pines.

Lago Maggiore is the second largest lake, 65km (40 miles) long and has wild, mountainous vistas to the north. The lakeside gardens burst with color in the spring when camellias, rhododendrons, and azaleas brighten the shores. Lago di Como is the deepest lake in Italy and is a popular inland spot for sailing. Speedboats carve through the deep blue waters as they zip between stylish towns on the shores of the lake.

TUSCANY

The classic image of the Tuscan landscape dotted with vines would not be complete without cypress trees lining the roads and crowning the hills. The cypress is traditionally associated with mortality and eternal spirituality, as the sweet-scented trees were once planted around cemeteries and their aromatic branches were buried with the dead. Today, this evergreen tree defines Tuscany's undulating landscape. Its tapering, cone-shaped form pierces the skyline, an image that endures in the memory of those who visit the region. Cypresses are often seen planted in rows,

extending for miles along wide avenues and meandering country roads around the Crete, La Foce, Monticiello, and Pienza. Although common in Tuscany they thrive throughout the country, benefiting from the warm Mediterranean climate. The largest and oldest cypress in Europe is in Soma in Lombardy. According to popular belief this massive 37-m high (120ft) specimen was planted around the time Christ was born.

Resembling the backdrop of a Renaissance painting, nowhere in Italy has inspired painters more than the countryside around Siena. This natural canvas of undulating fields is punctuated by the hilltop towns such as San Gimignano (above), whose red-tiled roofs glow orange at sunrise and continue to shimmer throughout the sunny summer days. In the fall, ploughs reveal a warm brown palette with rich red overtones, baked by the sun—the original 'Burnt Siena'. The pigment Burnt Siena comes from this Tuscan soil, *Terre di Siena*, a mixture of iron oxide and clay. This was one of the first painting pigments to be used by man and is found in many cave paintings. Naturally, the Renaissance painters found it the best medium with which to translate the rich colors and warmth of the Tuscan landscape on to canvas. Next page: The medieval city of Siena.

UMBRIA

Umbria, known as the green heart of Italy, is the only land-locked region in the country. Olive groves, fruit orchards, and wide stretches of woodland are punctuated by tall cypresses. In the middle of Italy, at the heart of hill country, its mountain towns, monasteries, and villages cling to the rugged hillsides. Umbria is famous for its painters and saints, and you can still walk along the paths they followed throughout the region. Pilgrims continue to flock to Assisi on the terraced slopes of Mount Subasio, which is the final resting place of St Francis and St Clare. The town has changed very little in the 700 years since these saints walked the cobbled streets among the pink stone quarried from the mountain.

Umbria's capital is the beautiful university city of Perugia. The fontana Maggiore (above) is in piazza IV Novembre, in front of the duomo.

NATURAL PHENOMENA

Mount Etna in Sicily (above and right) is 3,350m (11,000ft) high. As well as being Europe's largest live volcano it is one of the world's most active. It was believed by the Greeks to be the forge of Hephaestus, the god of fire, and it usually trails a plume of smoke, visible from most of the island.

Despite the frequent eruptions at Etna's crater, life goes on around the mountain's fertile slopes, with farmers harvesting bumper crops, particularly asparagus. Cleaning the ash from their cars and sweeping it out of the gutters is part of the weekly routine for residents.

Skiers can even whiz down its snowy upper slopes, which are home to some first-class ski resorts. The most popular among locals is the northern slope Piano Provenzana, as this side of Etna receives more snow. Adrenalin junkies and those who like to get close to the action prefer the pistes of

Linguaglossa, which means 'big tongue of lava'. These resorts understandably face unique problems—the last major eruption destroyed ski lifts and cable cars—but the passes are cheap and the skiing invigorating, with great views of the sea and a literal whiff of danger thrown in for free.

All that underground activity means that Italy is blessed with many mineral-rich, naturally-heated springs and there are *terme* (spas) all over the country. Mineral waters have long been used to treat everything from allergies and skin disorders to liver complaints, arthritis, and rheumatism.

Vesuvio, responsible for the destruction of Pompeii in AD79, last erupted in 1944 and it is overdue for another eruption. The danger lies not from the ash deposits or the lava flow, but from a surge of superheated, poisonous gas.

POMPEII

Pompeii is the world's best-preserved surviving Roman town, frozen in time by the catastrophic eruption of Vesuvio on 24 August AD79. The sudden flow of lava and superheated ash and gas that swept down the mountain captured a moment in time—women cooking, children playing, and men tilling the fields. As these have been

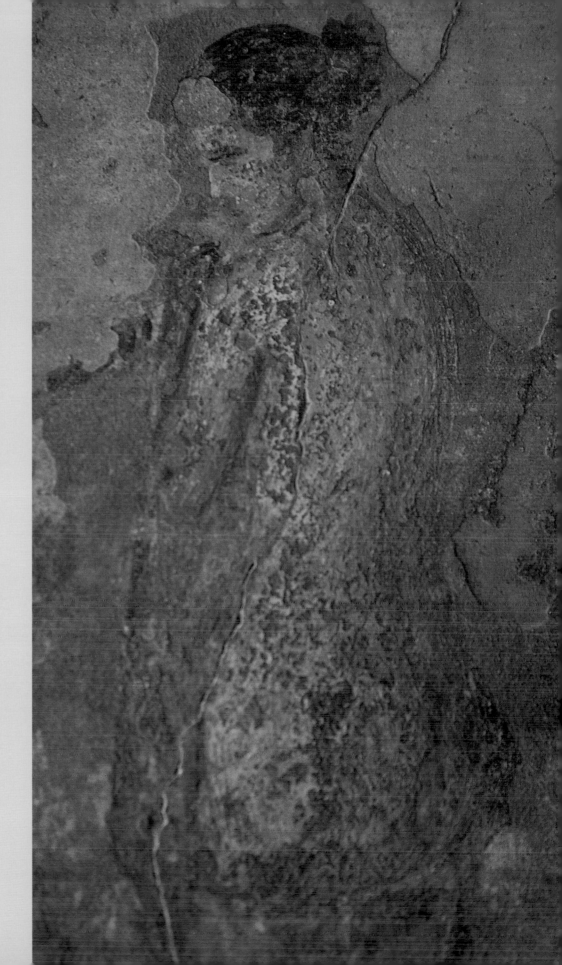

uncovered, archaeologists have been rewarded with a
unique glimpse into the past: Pompeii has yielded more
information about everyday Roman life and artistic
treasures than any other archaeological site in the world.

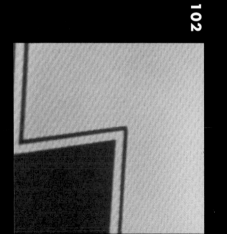

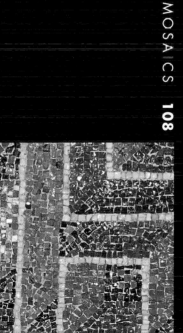

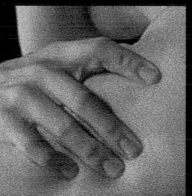

LA MODA

Italy has a long-established tradition of craftsmanship and luxurious living, dating back to the elaborate interior decoration of Roman villas and the glittering Renaissance palaces. With this background it is not surprising that fashion and design are booming. Italians infuse everything with style, whether it be clothes, fast cars or everyday household items.

Milan is one of the world's style capitals, filled with must-have fashion items and accessories by iconic labels such as Gucci, Armani, Prada, Missoni, and Versace, as well as bright and affordable wardrobes from Max Mara and Benetton. The Milanese may be trailblazers, eager to stand out from the crowd, but elsewhere the approach to clothes tends to be more conformist, with various rules of style followed by most people.

Refreshingly there is no pigeonholing of fashion designers within one industry and Italian style sets the standards and influences people across the globe—Donatella Versace has overseen every lifestyle element of the Italian-themed Palazzo Versace hotel in Australia, for example.

Could Prada be the new Palladio or Gucci the new Giotto? Perhaps it's not too fanciful to suggest that Italian fashion is the new art form. After all, the iconic Giorgio Armani exhibited his work at the Guggenheim Museum in New York in 2001 and Gianni Versace's creations were shown in the

Metropolitan Museum of Art in the same city in 2003. Italians have also recognized the skills of their native sons, with the Palazzo Pitti in Florence exhibiting more than 60 Gianfranco Ferre outfits during its grand re-opening.

Italians invest a great deal of time and effort into looking good. As the seasons and styles change, it is common for women to take a day off work to re-arrange their closet. Italians spend up to 50 percent of their disposable income on clothes and designer-wear is considered an option for all.

moretti

PRADA

DOLCE & GABBANA

VALENTINO
GARAVANI

VALENTINO
GARAVANI

OFFICIAL STYLE

Italy is renowned for its style on the football pitch. Known as the *Azzuri* (Blues), the national soccer side have consistently proved to be one of the world's top teams and are consistently the best turned out. Clubs are also defined by the color of their kit. Rome has two Serie A (premier league) soccer teams: Roma, known as the *Giallorossi* (Yellow-and-Reds), and Lazio, the *Biancocelesti* (White-and-Light-Blues).

If you understand the concept of *bella figura* you will understand the essence of Italian style. *Bella figura*, the preoccupation with appearance and innate sense of taste, is defined by presence, self-respect, and being careful not to let the side down. It's the image *carabinieri* (policemen) project when they lean against their Moto Guzzi motorbikes in jodhpurs and wraparound shades. It's not what you've got, but how you appear that counts.

The most famous scooter in Italy, the Vespa, owes its revolutionary construction and smooth lines to the aeronautic background of its designer, Corradino d'Ascanio. It was built and named by Enrico Piaggio—*'Sembra una vespa'* ('It looks like a wasp')—to meet postwar needs for an affordable means of transport for men and women, that kept their clothes clean. From humble beginnings it quickly became an icon, its elegantly simple look coming to symbolize a sense of freedom and independence for each new generation, thanks to careful adjustments to its design over the years.

Consequently it has been a scene-stealer in movies, from Fellini's *La Dolce Vita* right through to *Austin Powers' Goldmember*. Always trendsetters and keen to move with the times, the company Piaggio has branched out. It now produces a range of clothing and accessories to coordinate with its scooters.

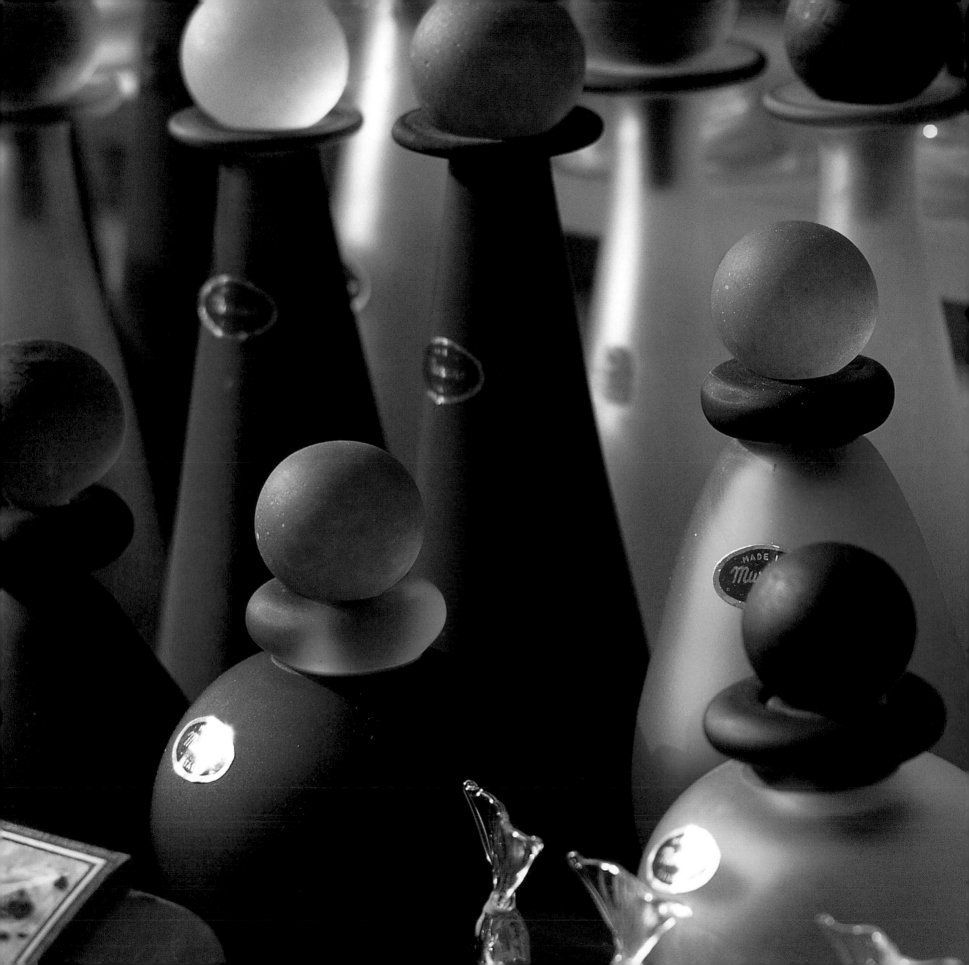

Previous page: The artisan tradition is alive and well and Murano glass from Venice is a prime example.

Once defined as painting for eternity, mosaics, such as those on display in the Musei Capitolini (above), were made using the same process employed today. Large sheets of glass, or thin slabs of marble, are first shattered into tiny pieces to make the *tesserae* (mosaic tiles). The surface on which the mosaic will be laid out is covered with a layer of cement and the outline of the image is traced on. A thin layer of mortar is then applied to the surface, on which a detailed painting of the final design is made. The pieces of glass and marble, set at fractionally different angles to refract the light, are then

MOSAICS

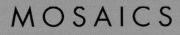

pressed into the wet mortar, creating an image that will endure for centuries. Renaissance painters and their patrons observed a rigid hierarchy of colors. It is easy to appreciate the value of the silver and gold pigments that enriched the altarpieces of the Middle Ages, pigments derived directly from the precious metals themselves, but few modern observers realize that ultramarine blue was just as valuable. Extracted from lapis lazuli, it was a costly Arabian import. Without lapis lazuli, many deep blue skies in Renaissance paintings, such as the luminous backdrop to Michelangelo's *Last Judgement* on the altar of the Sistine Chapel, would by now have faded to gray. The mosaics above are from the mausoleo di Galla Placidia in Ravenna. The city has so many valuable mosaics that they have been designated a Unesco World Heritage Site.

Michelangelo was commissioned by the city of Florence to carve the famous statue of David (above right) in 1501. It took the young sculptor three years to complete the Greek-inspired giant which he sculpted from a single block of marble. The statue, which shows David as he prepares to fight Goliath, quickly became a poignant symbol of republican liberty. It was designed to be viewed from below, and so David's long arms can look out of proportion to the rest of his body, further enhancing the powerful appearance of the figure. In preparation for David's 500th birthday in 2004, the statue was restored. The restoration project caused controversy, as efforts in previous centuries included cleansing with hydrochloric acid. The statue above left is by Gianbologna, while the sculpture opposite, which is in the Villa Borghese in Rome, is by Bernini.

LIGHT &
REFLECT

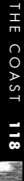

VENICE

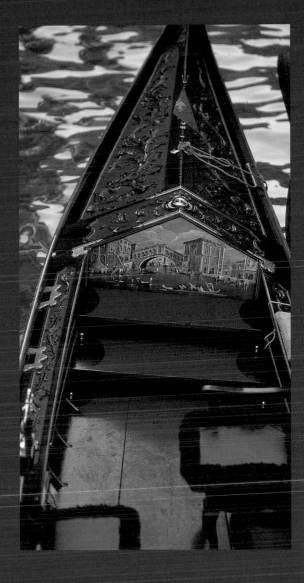

*S*itting on the edge of the lagoon watching the gondolas rocking up and down in their moorings and listening to the water lapping the edge of Piazza San Marco, it is easy to appreciate why Venice is one of the most romantic cities in the world.

The city is not perfect though, as it is shrouded in mist in winter and spring and plagued by the smell of stagnant water in the summer when the fierce sun beats down on the canals. But such is Venice's charm, and many people fall in love with the city, warts and all.

Businesses in Venice have learned to cope with the challenges of the city's rising waters and life carries on regardless. It is common to see seagulls paddling and children in gum boots having a whale of a time splashing around the tables and chairs of the elegant cafés bordering Piazza San Marco (right). This may be a charming image, but unfortunately Venice is sinking and this unique city, built on water, may disappear sooner than we think. Make sure you see it before the rising waters win and the city finally succumbs to a watery grave.

Venice has been battling against water for 1,500 years—it has sunk more than 23cm (9in) over the last 100 years—and scientists now estimate that unless dramatic action is taken, the city will be destroyed by the end of the century. Dedicated groups such as Venice in Peril and Save

Venice raise awareness and generate international support. The latest move by the Italian government is to install huge flood control barriers, a series of 78 mobile gates that can be used to control the water during high tides. The Moses Project, as it is known, is not without its critics. Environmentalists

claim it will disrupt the delicate balance in the lagoon and cause irreparable damage to the area's ecosystem.

THE COAST

The rising waters around Venice tend to hog the headlines, but Italy, a country surrounded by water, could lose 4,500sq km (1,740sq miles) of land to flooding and coastal erosion by the end of the century. Rapid development and erratic weather conditions in vulnerable areas have accelerated this

erosion. The sunny southern beaches are most at
risk, with the largest losses predicted between the
toe and heel of Italy around the Gulf of Taranto.
There are plans to build dikes to protect sensitive
areas and preserve some of the most beautiful and
dramatic sections of coastline.

SICILY

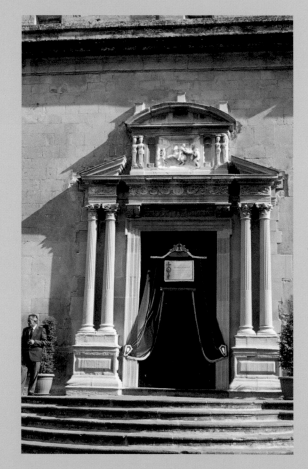

The island of Sicily embodies the essence of Italy. It's got it all: history and passion, beauty and romance, awe-inspiring artworks and architecture, crumbling ruins and crumbling buildings, fantastic food, rumbling volcanoes, striking beaches, bustling cities—and organized crime.

It lies to the southwest of mainland Italy's toe but after years of discussion, construction is due to start in 2005 on a suspension bridge that will cross the Straits of Messina, linking the two. The European Union has declined to help fund the project, so Italy has decided to finance the bridge

itself, aiming to complete the project by 2012 at a cost of €4.6 billion. The impressive structure is designed to resist earthquakes of up to 7.1 on the Richter scale and wind speeds of 200kph (125mph) and it will carry two railway lines and a 12-lane expressway. It will make it much easier to get to the island but officials are concerned that it will also bridge the gap between the Sicilian Mafia and Calabrian gangsters, making it harder to control the region's criminal activity.

Italian fountains are often theatrical affairs. Take the Fontana di Trevi in Rome (above) for example, immortalized by Federico Fellini's film *La Dolce Vita* when Anita Ekberg bathes in the water against the backdrop of busty baroque beauties, mythical creatures, nautical Greek gods, and headstrong horses riding on the crest of a wave. Fountains can be seen all over Rome, including in Piazza San Pietro (above left).

East of Rome is the watery paradise of Tivoli, resplendent with impressive aquatic displays and beautiful gardens. The ruins of Villa Adriana sprawl

FOUNTAINS

away from the town, nestling in olive groves. Begun in AD125, the villa covered an area as vast as the heart of imperial Rome. It was the largest and most costly palace ever built in the Empire, with bathhouses, temples, and a Greek theater—there was even a beach heated by steam pipes buried under the sand. The parkland is dotted with soothing pools and the Teatro Marittimo, a small palace thought to be the emperor Hadrian's private retreat, is on an island in the middle of an artificial lagoon. Villa d'Este (above), also in Tivoli, is famous for its fountains. Pirro Ligorio converted the former convent into a country retreat for Cardinal Ippolito d'Este, son of Lucrezia Borgia and the Duke of Ferrara, in 1550. The gardens are theatrical and elegant with water spouting from every corner and cascading down every surface.

Previous page: The Grotto del Buontalenti (1583–88) in the formal gardens of the Palazzo Pitti in Florence.

LIGHT & SHADE

Michelangelo Merisi, better known as Caravaggio (1573–1610), painted some of the best naturalistic paintings of the early 17th century. His most important contribution to the art world was through chiaroscuro, the dramatic use of contrasting light-and-dark effects that influenced successive generations of painters.

Caravaggio used models from the lower classes of society and re-created religious scenes, giving them an earthy, realistic resonance. He painted his subjects against a dark background illuminating them from a light source above their heads. His technique is so striking that it may appear slightly theatrical, but you only have to wander off the beaten track and explore the backstreets and watch the receding golden light casting angular shadows and leaving dark pools in corners, to appreciate where the artist found his inspiration.

TIME &
MOTION

COLORS OF ITALY: **TIME & MOTION** 7

ITALIA SPORTIVA

To Italians, keeping fit and looking good is crucial. Even the smallest town has a gym and there are sports appropriate to each season to keep people occupied—from swimming and water sports during the long, hot summers to ski-ing on the crisp white pistes in winter.

In such a varied country there is always something to get excited about and Italians display a level of energy and enthusiasm that spills over into all aspects of life. There is no shortage of festivals and events celebrating everything from spiritual holidays to gastronomic delights. For visitors these are a great opportunity to join in and feel part of the community.

Italy's best-loved spectator sport is soccer, which is followed passionately by millions of loyal fans. Hot on its heels in terms of popularity is basketball. The national team is now ranked among the best in the world. Baseball and American football have crept across the Atlantic and rugby is also beginning to make its mark, with interest growing since Italy's inclusion in the Six Nations Championship. However, motor racing and cycling are the sports which really get the nation's pulse racing.

track is a national passion. Italy's traditional racing color, fiery red, first used by Enzo Ferrari in the 1940s, is now synonymous with power, speed, and high performance and continues to dominate the Grand Prix in the popular imagination.
There are two Formula 1 Grand Prix races in Italy each year, the San Marino Grand Prix at Imola and the Italian Grand Prix at Monza, north of Milan. The latter is one of the highlights of the Formula 1 racing calendar, attracting a sea of red flag-waving supporters (above). Up close the cars zoom by in a blur, but the impression remains long after the checkered flag has been waved.

Next page: There is no shortage of spectators on Rome's streets during the annual city marathon.

The passion for football runs deep in Italy and dates back to Medieval times. Every year in June, Florence celebrates football's historic roots in its *Gioco di Calcio*, a no holds-barred version of football that is played between the four city quarters. Originally used to keep the city militia in fighting shape and to weld the various factions into a united force, it is understandably a rough-and-tumble affair. The beginning of the tournament is marked by a display of flag-throwing and ends with a costumed procession and candlelit boats and fireworks on the River Arno.

The crowds return year after year to Siena in July and August for the ultimate adrenaline rush of the *Palio*. The city is passionate about its centuries-old bareback horse race in Medieval costume round the main piazza, the Campo. The high speeds, confined space and lack of rules make it a hazardous and

exhilarating event. The race is over in minutes, but it takes weeks to prepare the pageantry, feasting, and staging that all add to the drama of the spectacle.

Further south in July, there are more historic costumes, horsemanship, and partying at *L'Ardia* *di San Costantino*, a dangerous downhill race in Sedilo, Sardinia. The race commemorates Constantine's victory in AD312 at the Battle of Ponte Milvio (Milvio Bridge), when Christianity was brought to Italy. Today's race re-creates the historic battle charge, with horses galloping full speed down a slope toward the finishing post, a fountain in the heart of town. A man representing Constantine heads the stampede and it is a safe bet who will win each year!

Next page: Two wheels are better than four when it comes to getting through city gridlock.

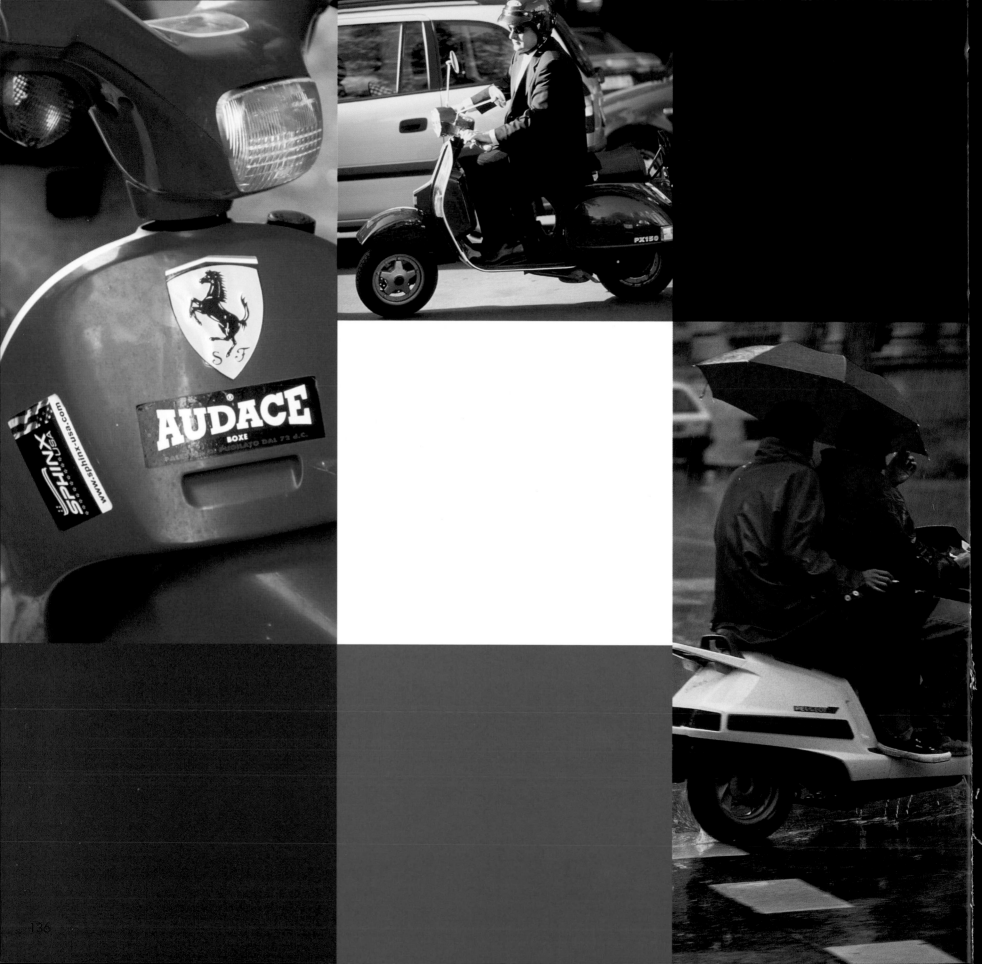

DUSK

Dusk is the perfect time to take a stroll and see Italy's famous sights in a whole new light. When the sun goes down, the lights are turned on and every square and street takes on a new aspect. Architectural details of famous monuments such as the Ponte Vecchio in Florence (left), the Colosseum, or St Peter's Basilica (above) in Rome are worth revisiting in the evening, while the narrow streets and midnight-blue canals of Venice, crowded during the day with visitors, become romantic and slightly spooky in the low light. Offices, museums, galleries, and shops shut down at the end of the day, but Rome never sleeps and things don't get going until well after the sun sets. There is plenty of nighttime activity as people gather to dine alfresco, have a quiet drink in a bar, or dance until dawn in a smoky club.
Next page: Santa Maria della Salute in Venice.

RIVA BOATS

With a long coastline, lakes and the canals of
Venice, Italians have embraced life on water. King
of the canals is the Riva speedboat, desired by
movie stars and magnates. Riva produces only 50 of
these exclusive boats a year, which have mahogany
trim, teak decks, and fine leather upholstery.

CATS

It is important to take some time out to relax and although the siesta has all but died out in the north, eventually the heat of the summer day halts proceedings. Cats never fail to take their afternoon nap and seem to embody the take-it-easy attitude that balances the frenetic activity of the city streets. They are often seen stretched out in the afternoon sun, absorbing heat from the paving slabs or shiny cars.

Large numbers of stray cats have made the streets of Rome their home, roaming ownerless around the city's archaeological sites and narrow alleyways.

Although they are easily distinguishable from the pampered apartment cats, and not as well groomed, the strays are far from neglected. Rome's legendary *gattare* (cat ladies) feed them, report illnesses to the city council vet, and provide them with comfort in the form of wooden cathouses.

CREDITS

The Automobile Association wishes to thank the following photo libraries for their assistance with the preparation of this project.

Photodisc 131t
Photo Courtesy of the Photo Library of Automobile Club Milano 131b

The remaining pictures are held in the Automobile Association's own photo library **(AA World Travel Library)** and were taken by the following photographers.

Jerry Edmanson 19bl, 31, 128bc, 134l; **Terry Harris** 29t, 36l, 36r, 39br, 50r, 60cl, 82/3, 90, 91, 127l; **Jim Henderson** 22bl, 40, 47l, 128br, 134c, 134r, 136br, 137br; **Max Jourdan** 5bcl, 12/3, 16, 24, 26tr, 28, 35cr, 35tr, 37, 42tr, 47r, 48, 50c, 51l, 53tl, 53br, 54tl, 54bl, 54br, 74r, 76cr, 77br, 82, 83r, 94, 94/5, 95, 96bc, 96br, 98r, 100l, 100bl, 100tr, 100c, 100br, 101tl, 101tr, 101c, 101br, 102, 103bl, 103cr, 105l, 108r, 112bc, 118l, 119cl, 119r, 129bc, 129br, 132/3, 135l, 135c, 135r, 137tl, 137tr, 142l, 143r; **Alex Kouprianoff** 4bl, 18bc, 23r, 42l, 60bc, 76bc, 80/1, 128bl, 130; **Simon McBride** 3tcr, 4bc, 5bl, 18br, 21br, 28/9, 38bl, 41t, 41b, 44/5, 49, 51r, 52/3, 52b, 53cl, 56bl, 57bc, 58, 59t, 59b, 61tl, 62/3, 64b, 67r, 69, 70/1, 73l, 73r, 77bl, 84l, 85, 97br, 99, 110l, 113bc, 116l, 116/7, 122l, 122r, 123, 126r, 136l, 136tc, 142r; **Dario Miterdiri** 4br, 14/5, 39bl, 52l, 57br, 61bl, 74l, 75, 111, 143l; **Rich Newton** 61c; **Ken Paterson** 3tl, 3tcl, 5bcr, 11l, 18bl, 19br, 21t, 21cl, 22br, 25, 30tr, 30b, 36c, 46l, 60tc, 60tr, 66l, 84r, 86, 87, 92t, 113br, 118br, 119bl, 127r; **Clive Sawyer** 3tr, 5br, 6, 8/9, 10bl, 11r, 17, 20, 22tl, 22tr, 23l, 26l, 26cl, 27br, 29b, 32/3, 34l, 34r, 38bc, 38br, 39bc, 42b, 43, 46r, 48/9, 50tl, 50bl, 54tr, 54bc, 55, 56bc, 56br, 57bl, 60bl, 61tr, 61br, 64tl, 64/5, 65, 66c, 66r, 67c, 68, 71, 72, 76bl, 77bc, 78l, 78r, 80, 90, 92b, 92/3, 96bl, 97bl, 98l, 103tl, 104, 105r, 106/7, 108l, 110r, 112bl, 112br, 113bl, 114, 115tl, 115bl, 115tr, 116r, 120t, 120l, 120c, 120r, 121, 124/5, 126l, 129bl, 138, 140/1, 144; **Tony Souter** 19bc, 27c, 30tl, 35l, 67l, 79, 97bc, 109t, 109b, 118tr, 119c; **Wyn Voysey** 26/7; **Peter Wilson** 10cr, 54ct, 139l, 139r.